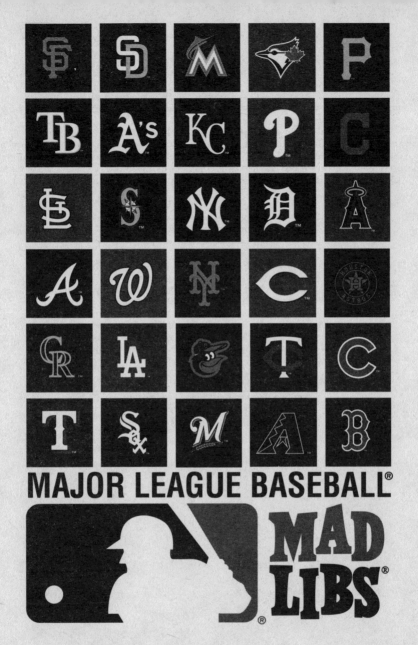

MAJOR LEAGUE BASEBALL®

MAD LIBS®

by Michael T. Riley

PSS!

PRICE STERN SLOAN

An Imprint of Penguin Random House

PRICE STERN SLOAN
Penguin Young Readers Group
An Imprint of Penguin Random House LLC

Major League Baseball trademarks and copyrights are used with permission
of Major League Baseball Properties, Inc. Visit MLB.com.
Used under license by Penguin Young Readers Group. All rights reserved.

Mad Libs format copyright © 2017 by Price Stern Sloan,
an imprint of Penguin Random House LLC. All rights reserved.

Concept created by Roger Price & Leonard Stern

Published by Price Stern Sloan,
an imprint of Penguin Random House LLC,
345 Hudson Street, New York, New York 10014.
Printed in the USA.

ISBN 9780451534019
1 3 5 7 9 10 8 6 4 2

MAD LIBS

INSTRUCTIONS

MAD LIBS® is a game for people who don't like games!
It can be played by one, two, three, four, or forty.

• RIDICULOUSLY SIMPLE DIRECTIONS

In this tablet you will find stories containing blank spaces where words
are left out. One player, the READER, selects one of these stories. The
READER does not tell anyone what the story is about. Instead, he/she asks
the other players, the WRITERS, to give him/her words. These words are
used to fill in the blank spaces in the story.

• TO PLAY

The READER asks each WRITER in turn to call out a word—an adjective or
a noun or whatever the space calls for—and uses them to fill in the blank
spaces in the story. The result is a MAD LIBS® game.

When the READER then reads the completed MAD LIBS® game to the other
players, they will discover that they have written a story that is fantastic,
screamingly funny, shocking, silly, crazy, or just plain dumb—depending
upon which words each WRITER called out.

• EXAMPLE (*Before* and *After*)

"_____!" he said _____
       EXCLAMATION   ADVERB

as he jumped into his convertible _____ and
                                           NOUN

drove off with his _____ wife.
                   ADJECTIVE

"_____**OUCH**_____!" he said _____**STUPIDLY**_____
       EXCLAMATION   ADVERB

as he jumped into his convertible _____**CAT**_____ and
                                           NOUN

drove off with his _____**BRAVE**_____ wife.
                   ADJECTIVE

In case you have forgotten what adjectives, adverbs, nouns, and verbs are, here is a quick review:

An ADJECTIVE describes something or somebody. *Lumpy, soft, ugly, messy,* and *short* are adjectives.

An ADVERB tells how something is done. It modifies a verb and usually ends in "ly." *Modestly, stupidly, greedily,* and *carefully* are adverbs.

A NOUN is the name of a person, place, or thing. *Sidewalk, umbrella, bridle, bathtub,* and *nose* are nouns.

A VERB is an action word. *Run, pitch, jump,* and *swim* are verbs. Put the verbs in past tense if the directions say PAST TENSE. *Ran, pitched, jumped,* and *swam* are verbs in the past tense.

When we ask for A PLACE, we mean any sort of place: a country or city (*Spain, Cleveland*) or a room (*bathroom, kitchen*).

An EXCLAMATION or SILLY WORD is any sort of funny sound, gasp, grunt, or outcry, like *Wow!, Ouch!, Whomp!, Ick!,* and *Gadzooks!*

When we ask for specific words, like a NUMBER, a COLOR, an ANIMAL, or a PART OF THE BODY, we mean a word that is one of those things, like *seven, blue, horse,* or *head.*

When we ask for a PLURAL, it means more than one. For example, *cat* pluralized is *cats.*

MAD LIBS® is fun to play with friends, but you can also play it by yourself! To begin with, DO NOT look at the story on the page below. Fill in the blanks on this page with the words called for. Then, using the words you have selected, fill in the blank spaces in the story.

Now you've created your own hilarious MAD LIBS® game!

SUITING UP

VERB _____

NOUN _____

ADJECTIVE _____

NUMBER _____

A PLACE _____

PERSON IN ROOM _____

ADJECTIVE _____

PART OF THE BODY _____

ARTICLE OF CLOTHING _____

COLOR _____

COLOR _____

VERB ENDING IN "ING" _____

ADVERB _____

ADJECTIVE _____

TYPE OF FOOD _____

NUMBER _____

NOUN _____

PART OF THE BODY _____

MAD LIBS

SUITING UP

No ballplayer should ever _____ onto the field looking

VERB

like he has slept under a/an _____. To make it in the

NOUN

_____ Leagues, you have to look sharp for the _____

ADJECTIVE   NUMBER

fans watching from (the) _____. The equipment manager,

A PLACE

_____, will provide you with a/an _____ helmet

PERSON IN ROOM   ADJECTIVE

to wear on your _____ when it's your turn to hit. Keep

PART OF THE BODY

your _____ tucked in, and match all accessories to

ARTICLE OF CLOTHING

your main uniform colors. _____ socks, a/an _____

COLOR   COLOR

undershirt, and _____ gloves are _____

VERB ENDING IN "ING"   ADVERB

recommended. You may become _____ for a snack during

ADJECTIVE

the game, but make sure your _____ stays tucked in your

TYPE OF FOOD

back pocket. And remember, safety should always be your number

_____ priority—make sure to wear a/an _____ on

NUMBER   NOUN

your _____ for protection!

PART OF THE BODY

MAD LIBS® is fun to play with friends, but you can also play it by yourself! To begin with, DO NOT look at the story on the page below. Fill in the blanks on this page with the words called for. Then, using the words you have selected, fill in the blank spaces in the story.

Now you've created your own hilarious MAD LIBS® game!

LIVE FROM THE BROADCAST BOOTH

SILLY WORD _____

PLURAL NOUN _____

NOUN _____

ADJECTIVE _____

ANIMAL _____

ADJECTIVE _____

PERSON IN ROOM _____

PLURAL NOUN _____

NOUN _____

NOUN _____

VERB ENDING IN "ING" _____

VERB _____

NOUN _____

ADJECTIVE _____

PLURAL NOUN _____

NOUN _____

NOUN _____

MAD LIBS®
LIVE FROM THE
BROADCAST BOOTH

Good afternoon baseball fans! Welcome to historic _____

SILLY WORD

Park, home of the Boston Red _____ and the famous

PLURAL NOUN

"Green _____," for what promises to be a/an _____

NOUN   _ADJECTIVE_

Game Seven of the American League Championship Series. I'm Joe

_____, calling the action alongside my _____

ANIMAL   _ADJECTIVE_

colleague, _____. This one is for all the _____,

PERSON IN ROOM   _PLURAL NOUN_

as the winner punches a/an _____ all the way to the World

NOUN

Series! So far, home _____ advantage has been key. These

NOUN

fans have been _____ so loud I can hardly hear myself

VERB ENDING IN "ING"

_____! On the mound today is a pitcher nicknamed "The

VERB

_____" for his devastating split-finger _____-ball.

NOUN   _ADJECTIVE_

He's going to need it today against this lineup, which led the league

in _____ this season. All the excitement is right around

PLURAL NOUN

the _____, so don't touch that _____! We'll be back

NOUN   _NOUN_

after this.

MAD LIBS® is fun to play with friends, but you can also play it by yourself! To begin with, DO NOT look at the story on the page below. Fill in the blanks on this page with the words called for. Then, using the words you have selected, fill in the blank spaces in the story.

Now you've created your own hilarious MAD LIBS® game!

VALUABLE HITTING ADVICE

ADJECTIVE _____

NOUN _____

PLURAL NOUN _____

PART OF THE BODY _____

A PLACE _____

VERB _____

NUMBER _____

ADJECTIVE _____

NOUN _____

ADJECTIVE _____

NOUN _____

NOUN _____

PERSON IN ROOM _____

NOUN _____

FIRST NAME (FEMALE) _____

COLOR _____

VERB _____

SAME VERB _____

MAD LIBS®
VALUABLE HITTING
ADVICE

One of the most _____ tasks in all of sports is hitting a ball
<small>ADJECTIVE</small>

the size of a/an _____ with a bat, especially when a pitcher
<small>NOUN</small>

is throwing it over 100 _____ per hour. It requires precise
<small>PLURAL NOUN</small>

timing and hand-_____ coordination. Many young hitters
<small>PART OF THE BODY</small>

swing too hard, trying to hit the ball out of (the) _____,
<small>A PLACE</small>

and _____ for strike _____. The best hitters keep
<small>VERB</small>   <small>NUMBER</small>

a/an _____ grip on the _____ and focus on making
<small>ADJECTIVE</small>   <small>NOUN</small>

contact with the _____ spot. Stance is also important.
<small>ADJECTIVE</small>

Position yourself about half the length of a/an _____
<small>NOUN</small>

from home _____ and tilt your head sideways to stare
<small>NOUN</small>

down _____. Be selective! A walk is just as good as a/an
<small>PERSON IN ROOM</small>

_____. And remember, the greatest legends, from Babe
<small>NOUN</small>

_____ to Paul _____-schmidt, have all struck
<small>FIRST NAME (FEMALE)</small>   <small>COLOR</small>

out. If at first you don't succeed, _____ and _____
<small>VERB</small>   <small>SAME VERB</small>

again.

From MLB MAD LIBS® • ™ and © Major League Baseball Properties, Inc. Published in 2017 by Price Stern Sloan,
an imprint of Penguin Random House LLC, 345 Hudson Street, New York, NY 10014.

MAD LIBS® is fun to play with friends, but you can also play it by yourself! To begin with, DO NOT look at the story on the page below. Fill in the blanks on this page with the words called for. Then, using the words you have selected, fill in the blank spaces in the story.

Now you've created your own hilarious MAD LIBS® game!

GOING...GOING...GONE!

NOUN _____

ADJECTIVE _____

PLURAL NOUN _____

PLURAL NOUN _____

ADJECTIVE _____

NOUN _____

NOUN _____

PLURAL NOUN _____

NOUN _____

NOUN _____

A PLACE _____

NOUN _____

COLOR _____

ADJECTIVE _____

PLURAL NOUN _____

NOUN _____

PLURAL NOUN _____

ADVERB _____

MAD LIBS®
GOING . . . GOING . . . GONE!

The sight of a crushed baseball soaring through the sky like a shooting

_____ can only be described as _____. Sluggers
NOUN   ADJECTIVE

like Josh Donaldson and Chris Davis clear the _____
                                                       PLURAL NOUN

with one mighty swing of their _____, launching the ball
                                         PLURAL NOUN

into the _____ seats of the upper _____, or farther!
            ADJECTIVE   NOUN

Cubs All-Star Kris Bryant once blasted a home run _____
                                                          NOUN

an astonishing 495 _____, putting a dent in the
                             PLURAL NOUN

Wrigley Field _____ the size of a/an _____! When
               NOUN   NOUN

Giancarlo Stanton hits, every car in (the) _____ is in danger
                                         A PLACE

of getting its _____ shattered! Players who hit moonshots
                        NOUN

often win the _____ Slugger Award or are named Most
                     COLOR

_____ Player, and are showcased on top ten countdowns for
ADJECTIVE

the _____ of the day. Of course, nothing beats a walk-off
               PLURAL NOUN

shot, when players circle the _____ ready to shower their
                                 NOUN

teammate with _____ as the announcer declares to the
                        PLURAL NOUN

fans, "Drive home _____!"
                      ADVERB

From MLB MAD LIBS® • ™ and © Major League Baseball Properties, Inc. Published in 2017 by Price Stern Sloan,
an imprint of Penguin Random House LLC, 345 Hudson Street, New York, NY 10014.

MAD LIBS® is fun to play with friends, but you can also play it by yourself! To begin with, DO NOT look at the story on the page below. Fill in the blanks on this page with the words called for. Then, using the words you have selected, fill in the blank spaces in the story.

Now you've created your own hilarious MAD LIBS® game!

CLUBHOUSE ETIQUETTE

ADJECTIVE _____

ADJECTIVE _____

NOUN _____

NUMBER _____

PLURAL NOUN _____

ANIMAL _____

LETTER OF THE ALPHABET _____

PART OF THE BODY _____

CELEBRITY _____

NOUN _____

PART OF THE BODY _____

NOUN _____

ADJECTIVE _____

NOUN _____

PERSON IN ROOM _____

NOUN _____

SILLY WORD _____

MAD LIBS
CLUBHOUSE
ETIQUETTE

Welcome to the show, rookie! Here are some _____ tips for
                                              ADJECTIVE
young players still _____ behind the ears:
                        ADJECTIVE

1. Don't be late! Set your alarm _____ to ring at least
                                      NOUN
_____ hours before practice.
   NUMBER

2. Rookie pitchers carry all the bags of _____ to the
                                            PLURAL NOUN
_____ pen for warm-ups.
   ANIMAL

3. You may have been vocal in Triple-_____, but in the
                                   LETTER OF THE ALPHABET
Majors you'll need to bite your _____ and speak only when
                                 PART OF THE BODY
spoken to.

4. Hands off the clubhouse stereo! Listen to _____'s holiday
                                                CELEBRITY
album on your i-_____ (with _____-phones, of course).
                  NOUN   PART OF THE BODY

5. Wash your _____ daily unless you want your locker to
                 NOUN
smell _____.
      ADJECTIVE

6. Write your name on your _____ so _____
                              NOUN   PERSON IN ROOM
doesn't shower with it (by accident, at least).

7. Watch your language! Don't yell "Holy _____!" or use
                                            NOUN
words like _____ in front of reporters.
              SILLY WORD

MAD LIBS® is fun to play with friends, but you can also play it by yourself! To begin with, DO NOT look at the story on the page below. Fill in the blanks on this page with the words called for. Then, using the words you have selected, fill in the blank spaces in the story.

Now you've created your own hilarious MAD LIBS® game!

BUY ME SOME PEANUTS AND . . . TACO DOGS???

ADJECTIVE _____

NOUN _____

ADJECTIVE _____

ADJECTIVE _____

NOUN _____

ADJECTIVE _____

A PLACE _____

ADJECTIVE _____

PART OF THE BODY _____

NOUN _____

PLURAL NOUN _____

NOUN _____

NOUN _____

ARTICLE OF CLOTHING _____

TYPE OF FOOD _____

TYPE OF LIQUID _____

MAD☺LIBS®
BUY ME SOME PEANUTS
AND ... TACO DOGS???

We've scoured each Major League ballpark to create this

_____ menu of the weirdest, wackiest ballpark delicacies:
  ADJECTIVE

Fried Corn on the _____ **(Rangers):** *Vegetables are always*
                NOUN

_____, *unless they're deep-fried!*
  ADJECTIVE

Tachos (Pirates): *A pub favorite, only with* _____ *potatoes.*
                             ADJECTIVE

Enjoy with your hands or with a/an _____.
                            NOUN

Taco Dogs (Rockies): *An old-time classic with a little* _____
                                   ADJECTIVE

spice. This combo brings the flavor of (the) _____ *to your*
                                 A PLACE

_____-*dog bun.*
  ADJECTIVE

Chicken & Waffle Cone (Astros): *With this portable treat, eat dinner*

with one _____ *and wear a foam* _____ *on the other!*
    PART OF THE BODY   NOUN

Fan versus Food Burger (Rays): *If you finish, you win two free*

_____ *for the next game—that is, if you can still lift yourself*
  PLURAL NOUN

out of your _____!
              NOUN

Four-Pound Banana Split (White Sox): *Twelve scoops of vanilla*

_____ *served in a life-size batter's* _____ *and*
  NOUN   ARTICLE OF CLOTHING

drizzled with _____ *sauce and chocolate* _____!
          TYPE OF FOOD   TYPE OF LIQUID

MAD LIBS® is fun to play with friends, but you can also play it by yourself! To begin with, DO NOT look at the story on the page below. Fill in the blanks on this page with the words called for. Then, using the words you have selected, fill in the blank spaces in the story.

Now you've created your own hilarious MAD LIBS® game!

HOME SWEET HOME

ADJECTIVE _____

ADJECTIVE _____

ADJECTIVE _____

PLURAL NOUN _____

NOUN _____

PLURAL NOUN _____

PLURAL NOUN _____

PLURAL NOUN _____

NOUN _____

TYPE OF FOOD _____

NOUN _____

PLURAL NOUN _____

TYPE OF LIQUID _____

NOUN _____

PLURAL NOUN _____

PLURAL NOUN _____

LAST NAME _____

MAD LIBS
HOME SWEET HOME

A/An _____ stadium is essential for giving its home team an
     ADJECTIVE

edge and keeping fans _____. Some ballparks stir memories
                 ADJECTIVE

of our national pastime's _____ days, like Wrigley Field,
                ADJECTIVE

where _____ get lost in the _____ growing on the
   PLURAL NOUN   NOUN

outfield walls. More state-of-the-art venues boast fancier features, like

high-definition _____! A museum at Marlins Park displays
       PLURAL NOUN

hundreds of bobblehead _____ representing baseball's all-
           PLURAL NOUN

time greatest _____ inside a massive glass _____.
     PLURAL NOUN   NOUN

At Citi Field, a giant _____ rises up when any Mets batter
         TYPE OF FOOD

blasts a home _____. When Angels sluggers round the
      NOUN

_____, a center-field geyser shoots _____
 PLURAL NOUN   TYPE OF LIQUID

into the air. Sometimes the thrills are in the surroundings. The view

of the St. Louis _____ from Busch Stadium is breathtaking,
       NOUN

while in San Francisco, fans float around in _____ waiting
                    PLURAL NOUN

for _____ to splash into _____ Cove.
  PLURAL NOUN   LAST NAME

From MLB MAD LIBS® • ™ and © Major League Baseball Properties, Inc. Published in 2017 by Price Stern Sloan,
an imprint of Penguin Random House LLC, 345 Hudson Street, New York, NY 10014.

MAD LIBS® is fun to play with friends, but you can also play it by yourself! To begin with, DO NOT look at the story on the page below. Fill in the blanks on this page with the words called for. Then, using the words you have selected, fill in the blank spaces in the story.

Now you've created your own hilarious MAD LIBS® game!

OCTOBER MAGIC

ADJECTIVE _____

NOUN _____

ANIMAL _____

FIRST NAME (MALE) _____

NOUN _____

PERSON IN ROOM _____

ADJECTIVE _____

PLURAL NOUN _____

VERB _____

ADJECTIVE _____

PLURAL NOUN _____

A PLACE _____

VERB _____

COLOR _____

ADJECTIVE _____

ADVERB _____

PART OF THE BODY _____

In the _____ October air, every _____ is magnified
           ADJECTIVE   NOUN

and the anticipation for each pitch feels like a/an _____
                                                        ANIMAL

in the stomach. A postseason run can transform an average

_____ into a household _____ overnight, just like
FIRST NAME (MALE)   NOUN

_____. Recently, it seems the Giants find a new hero every
PERSON IN ROOM

_____ year. However, the game's brightest _____
   ADJECTIVE   PLURAL NOUN

typically _____ to the occasion. Look no further than Derek
              VERB

Jeter, whose _____ flip to home plate in 2001 legitimized his
                 ADJECTIVE

role as captain of the New York _____. Joe Carter became
                                    PLURAL NOUN

a hero in (the) _____ when his _____-off blast
                   A PLACE   VERB

won the World Series for the 1993 _____ Jays. And Dodgers
                                       COLOR

fans still imitate Kirk Gibson's _____ moment from 1988,
                                     ADJECTIVE

when he trotted around the bases _____ pumping his
                                      ADVERB

_____.
PART OF THE BODY

MAD LIBS® is fun to play with friends, but you can also play it by yourself! To begin with, DO NOT look at the story on the page below. Fill in the blanks on this page with the words called for. Then, using the words you have selected, fill in the blank spaces in the story.

Now you've created your own hilarious MAD LIBS® game!

CAN'T WE ALL JUST GET ALONG?

ADJECTIVE _____

COLOR _____

NOUN _____

NOUN _____

CELEBRITY _____

NOUN _____

TYPE OF LIQUID _____

PLURAL NOUN _____

PART OF THE BODY _____

TYPE OF LIQUID _____

PLURAL NOUN _____

NOUN _____

PLURAL NOUN _____

NOUN _____

COLOR _____

NOUN _____

ADJECTIVE _____

NOUN _____

MAD LIBS
CAN'T WE ALL JUST GET ALONG?

There is no love lost between baseball's most _____ rivalries.

ADJECTIVE

The Yankees and _____ Sox compete tooth and _____

COLOR · NOUN

in the American League _____ division. Boston fans blamed

NOUN

New York's dominance on the "Curse of _____" until 2004,

CELEBRITY

when Curt Schilling's _____ was famously stained with

NOUN

_____. The Sox turned the _____ on their rivals, but

TYPE OF LIQUID · PLURAL NOUN

soon after, Johnny Damon shaved his _____ and left to join

PART OF THE BODY

the Yanks. In the National League, the Cubs and Cardinals are like oil

and _____. Separated by three hundred _____,

TYPE OF LIQUID · PLURAL NOUN

these franchises divide the Midwest during the _____ race.

NOUN

The Cards boast many championship _____ while the

PLURAL NOUN

Cubs earned a/an _____ in their cap in 2015, bouncing the

NOUN

_____-birds from the playoffs. The Giants and Dodgers

COLOR

agree the NL West is best—but that's about the only _____

NOUN

they agree on! When these foes battle, expect a/an _____

ADJECTIVE

sound when the ball lands in the catcher's _____.

NOUN

From MLB MAD LIBS® • ™ and © Major League Baseball Properties, Inc. Published in 2017 by Price Stern Sloan, an imprint of Penguin Random House LLC, 345 Hudson Street, New York, NY 10014.

MAD LIBS® is fun to play with friends, but you can also play it by yourself! To begin with, DO NOT look at the story on the page below. Fill in the blanks on this page with the words called for. Then, using the words you have selected, fill in the blank spaces in the story.

Now you've created your own hilarious MAD LIBS® game!

LEARNING THE LINGO

NOUN _____

ADJECTIVE _____

PLURAL NOUN _____

ADJECTIVE _____

A PLACE _____

PLURAL NOUN _____

ADJECTIVE _____

NOUN _____

NOUN _____

ADJECTIVE _____

NOUN _____

VERB _____

NOUN _____

VERB ENDING IN "ING" _____

PLURAL NOUN _____

MAD LIBS®

LEARNING THE LINGO

So, your best friend loves the Arizona _____-backs, but to
NOUN

you, baseball seems like some _____ ritual performed by
ADJECTIVE

_____. Just memorize this helpful guide and train your
PLURAL NOUN

baseball brain to be as _____ as an umpire!
ADJECTIVE

Infield fly: If a batter hits a pop-up to (the) _____ with
A PLACE

_____ on first and second, the batter is automatically
PLURAL NOUN

_____.
ADJECTIVE

Tagging up: Once a fly ball hits a fielder's _____, the
NOUN

runner may try to advance, so long as he first touches the original

_____.
NOUN

Ground-rule double: A/An _____ base hit that bounces over
ADJECTIVE

the outfield _____.
NOUN

Check swing: When the batter starts to _____ but holds his
VERB

_____ back before committing.
NOUN

Force play: _____ the runner is not necessary.
VERB ENDING IN "ING"

Full count: The pitcher has thrown the maximum amount of balls

and _____.
PLURAL NOUN

MAD LIBS® is fun to play with friends, but you can also play it by yourself! To begin with, DO NOT look at the story on the page below. Fill in the blanks on this page with the words called for. Then, using the words you have selected, fill in the blank spaces in the story.

Now you've created your own hilarious MAD LIBS® game!

FAN TRADITIONS

PLURAL NOUN _____

COLOR _____

PLURAL NOUN _____

PLURAL NOUN _____

NOUN _____

A PLACE _____

ADJECTIVE _____

PLURAL NOUN _____

ANIMAL _____

NOUN _____

NOUN _____

ADJECTIVE _____

FIRST NAME (FEMALE) _____

FIRST NAME (MALE) _____

TYPE OF FOOD _____

ANIMAL _____

MAD LIBS®
FAN TRADITIONS

From singing to banging souvenir _____ together to
<small>PLURAL NOUN</small>

waving _____ rally _____, every city has a unique
<small>COLOR</small> <small>PLURAL NOUN</small>

way of supporting its team. Atlanta Braves faithful do The Tomahawk

Chop, swinging foam _____ as they chant along to war
<small>PLURAL NOUN</small>

music playing on a/an _____. If you visit the Los Angeles
<small>NOUN</small>

Angels of (the) _____, you'll hear the _____ sound
<small>A PLACE</small> <small>ADJECTIVE</small>

of colliding Thunder _____, as the Rally _____,
<small>PLURAL NOUN</small> <small>ANIMAL</small>

their beloved primate, holds up a sign declaring "It's _____
<small>NOUN</small>

Time!" In Baltimore, "Thank God I'm a Country _____" gets
<small>NOUN</small>

the locals roaring with approval, while good times have never seemed

so _____ when Boston fans sing "Sweet _____"
<small>ADJECTIVE</small> <small>FIRST NAME (FEMALE)</small>

by _____ Diamond. In Washington, cheering on mascot
<small>FIRST NAME (MALE)</small>

Teddy Roosevelt while he races against his presidential counterparts

is a tradition as American as apple _____ and the bald
<small>TYPE OF FOOD</small>

_____.
<small>ANIMAL</small>

From MLB MAD LIBS® • ™ and © Major League Baseball Properties, Inc. Published in 2017 by Price Stern Sloan, an imprint of Penguin Random House LLC, 345 Hudson Street, New York, NY 10014.

MAD LIBS® is fun to play with friends, but you can also play it by yourself! To begin with, DO NOT look at the story on the page below. Fill in the blanks on this page with the words called for. Then, using the words you have selected, fill in the blank spaces in the story.

Now you've created your own hilarious MAD LIBS® game!

BASEBALL HISTORY BY THE NUMBERS

ADJECTIVE _____

ADJECTIVE _____

NOUN _____

PLURAL NOUN _____

NOUN _____

PLURAL NOUN _____

NOUN _____

NOUN _____

ADJECTIVE _____

VERB ENDING IN "ING" _____

ADJECTIVE _____

ADJECTIVE _____

NOUN _____

PLURAL NOUN _____

NOUN _____

ADJECTIVE _____

A PLACE _____

Cal Ripken Jr. never called in _____ or missed time on the
ADJECTIVE

_____ list. He surpassed "The Iron _____" Lou
ADJECTIVE ___NOUN___

Gehrig with 2,632 consecutive _____ played. Ripken's record
PLURAL NOUN

and Joe DiMaggio's 56 straight games with a/an _____ are
NOUN

streaks that are sure to stand the test of time. Both these legends

compiled enough _____ batted in to make the Hall of
PLURAL NOUN

_____, but not more than Hank Aaron, who for decades
NOUN

also ruled as the all-time _____ king. Many would argue,
NOUN

however, that the most truly _____ record is .366, the career
ADJECTIVE

_____ average of the _____ Ty Cobb. Cobb
VERB ENDING IN "ING" _ADJECTIVE_

was a/an _____-nosed player who feared no one, although
ADJECTIVE

he never faced Nolan Ryan. "The _____ Express" threw
NOUN

no-hitters for three different _____—seven altogether—
PLURAL NOUN

before taking his final steps off the pitcher's _____. Records
NOUN

are made to be _____, but these might just stand until (the)
ADJECTIVE

_____ freezes over!
A PLACE

From MLB MAD LIBS® • ™ and © Major League Baseball Properties, Inc. Published in 2017 by Price Stern Sloan,
an imprint of Penguin Random House LLC, 345 Hudson Street, New York, NY 10014.

MAD LIBS® is fun to play with friends, but you can also play it by yourself! To begin with, DO NOT look at the story on the page below. Fill in the blanks on this page with the words called for. Then, using the words you have selected, fill in the blank spaces in the story.

Now you've created your own hilarious MAD LIBS® game!

FAMOUS FANS

LETTER OF THE ALPHABET _____

PLURAL NOUN _____

ADJECTIVE _____

NOUN _____

ADJECTIVE _____

FIRST NAME (MALE) _____

NOUN _____

A PLACE _____

NOUN _____

PLURAL NOUN _____

PLURAL NOUN _____

VERB ENDING IN "ING" _____

NOUN _____

COLOR _____

NOUN _____

NOUN _____

MAD LIBS

FAMOUS FANS

_____-list celebrities always wear their baseball loyalty
<u>LETTER OF THE ALPHABET</u>

on their _____. The host of *The Price Is* _____,
<u>PLURAL NOUN</u> <u>ADJECTIVE</u>

Drew Carey, trumpets his Indians fandom, much like Cubs fan Bill

Murray, star of _____-*busters*. Rap icon Nelly may think
<u>NOUN</u>

"it's getting _____ in here," but he won't take off his St.
<u>ADJECTIVE</u>

_____ Cardinals jersey. Kid _____ backs the
<u>FIRST NAME (MALE)</u> <u>NOUN</u>

Detroit Tigers, even while singing "Sweet Home _____"
<u>A PLACE</u>

all summer long. It's always summer in L.A., where former *Who's the*

_____ star Alyssa Milano supports the Dodgers. Stephen
<u>NOUN</u>

King has penned books about killer _____, haunted
<u>PLURAL NOUN</u>

_____, and his beloved Red Sox. Comedian Billy Crystal
<u>PLURAL NOUN</u>

actually batted for the Yankees in a Spring _____
<u>VERB ENDING IN "ING"</u>

game, while funnyman Jerry Seinfeld loves their cross-_____
<u>NOUN</u>

rivals, the Mets. When he was in the _____ House, fellow
<u>COLOR</u>

White Sox fans sang "Hail to the _____" for Barack Obama
<u>NOUN</u>

whenever he threw out the first _____.
<u>NOUN</u>

From MLB MAD LIBS® • ™ and © Major League Baseball Properties, Inc. Published in 2017 by Price Stern Sloan,
an imprint of Penguin Random House LLC, 345 Hudson Street, New York, NY 10014.

MAD LIBS® is fun to play with friends, but you can also play it by yourself! To begin with, DO NOT look at the story on the page below. Fill in the blanks on this page with the words called for. Then, using the words you have selected, fill in the blank spaces in the story.

Now you've created your own hilarious MAD LIBS® game!

TRADING PLACES

NOUN _____

NUMBER _____

SILLY WORD _____

NOUN _____

COLOR _____

PLURAL NOUN _____

NOUN _____

OCCUPATION _____

ADVERB _____

NOUN _____

A PLACE _____

LAST NAME _____

PART OF THE BODY _____

NOUN _____

PLURAL NOUN _____

NOUN _____

ANIMAL _____

NOUN _____

MAD LIBS®

TRADING PLACES

You were an indispensible part of your team's _____.

NOUN

For years, you gave nothing less than _____ percent. Fans

NUMBER

chanted your name, screaming out "Let's go _____!" The

SILLY WORD

ballpark sold out on your souvenir _____ day. Last year,

NOUN

you won the _____ Glove Award and were on the cover of

COLOR

_____ Illustrated. But your cell _____ just rang.

PLURAL NOUN   NOUN

It was the team's _____, who _____ said you've

OCCUPATION   ADVERB

been traded for a/an _____ to be named later! You've never

NOUN

even been to (the) _____, but now you have to help their team

A PLACE

win the _____ Trophy. You called your agent, Seymour

LAST NAME

_____. He said your contract has a no-_____

PART OF THE BODY   NOUN

clause, but it doesn't say anything about trades. So you'll have to pack

your belongings, leave only your _____ behind, and rent

PLURAL NOUN

an apartment in the _____ District of your new city. The

NOUN

restaurants there serve great fried _____, so maybe you can

ANIMAL

re-sign next year as a free _____ after all!

NOUN

MAD LIBS® is fun to play with friends, but you can also play it by yourself! To begin with, DO NOT look at the story on the page below. Fill in the blanks on this page with the words called for. Then, using the words you have selected, fill in the blank spaces in the story.

Now you've created your own hilarious MAD LIBS® game!

THE THRILL OF THEFT

ADJECTIVE _____

NOUN _____

PLURAL NOUN _____

PART OF THE BODY _____

NOUN _____

NOUN _____

PLURAL NOUN _____

A PLACE _____

ARTICLE OF CLOTHING _____

NOUN _____

ANIMAL _____

ADJECTIVE _____

ADJECTIVE _____

ADJECTIVE _____

PART OF THE BODY _____

ADJECTIVE _____

MAD LIBS

THE THRILL OF THEFT

Nothing makes a pitcher more nervous than a/an _____
ADJECTIVE

runner. Teams with speedsters at the top of their _____ can
NOUN

manufacture _____ using little to no power. Hall of Famers
PLURAL NOUN

Rickey Henderson and Lou Brock could sprint ninety feet in the blink

of a/an _____. For others, swiping a/an _____
PART OF THE BODY   NOUN

is all about timing. A runner must take a lead the length of a/an

_____, then study the pitcher's _____. The third
NOUN   PLURAL NOUN

base coach relays signals from (the) _____ by tugging on his
A PLACE

_____, indicating when it's time to run. You can cut
ARTICLE OF CLOTHING

the tension with a/an _____ as the runner sprints like a/an
NOUN

_____ across the _____ infield dirt. If the catcher's
ANIMAL   ADJECTIVE

throw is _____, the second baseman or _____-stop
ADJECTIVE   ADJECTIVE

will put a tag down. Sometimes, a/an _____-first slide is the
PART OF THE BODY

only way to avoid hearing the umpire yell, "You're _____!"
ADJECTIVE

From MLB MAD LIBS® • ™ and © Major League Baseball Properties, Inc. Published in 2017 by Price Stern Sloan, an imprint of Penguin Random House LLC, 345 Hudson Street, New York, NY 10014.

MAD LIBS® is fun to play with friends, but you can also play it by yourself! To begin with, DO NOT look at the story on the page below. Fill in the blanks on this page with the words called for. Then, using the words you have selected, fill in the blank spaces in the story.

Now you've created your own hilarious MAD LIBS® game!

THE BABE

PLURAL NOUN _____

ADJECTIVE _____

NOUN _____

NOUN _____

NOUN _____

NUMBER _____

NUMBER _____

NOUN _____

NOUN _____

NOUN _____

NOUN _____

NOUN _____

ADJECTIVE _____

NOUN _____

ADJECTIVE _____

ADJECTIVE _____

PLURAL NOUN _____

MAD LIBS

THE BABE

Eighty _____ after his retirement, the "_____
         PLURAL NOUN   ADJECTIVE

Bambino" Babe Ruth is still considered the most legendary _____
                                                                    NOUN

in baseball history. At first a pitcher, his knack for clubbing the long-

_____ earned him the nickname "Sultan of _____."
      NOUN   NOUN

For decades, Ruth's totals of _____ and _____ stood as
                                    NUMBER   NUMBER

records for number of home runs in a season and a career. Legend

has it, during the 1932 _____ Series, Ruth brazenly called
                               NOUN

his _____ by pointing his bat toward the _____
          NOUN   NOUN

in center field. The Babe became so larger-than-_____ that
                                                        NOUN

Yankee Stadium was dubbed "The _____ that Ruth Built."
                                        NOUN

In 1927, he headlined a lineup so _____ that enthusiasts
                                         ADJECTIVE

called it "Murderers' _____." When you consider some of his
                            NOUN

_____ training methods, his _____ athleticism
     ADJECTIVE   ADJECTIVE

was astounding. And to think, the Red Sox basically sold him to the

Yankees for a bag of _____!
                          PLURAL NOUN

From MLB MAD LIBS® • ™ and © Major League Baseball Properties, Inc. Published in 2017 by Price Stern Sloan, an imprint of Penguin Random House LLC, 345 Hudson Street, New York, NY 10014.

MAD LIBS® is fun to play with friends, but you can also play it by yourself! To begin with, DO NOT look at the story on the page below. Fill in the blanks on this page with the words called for. Then, using the words you have selected, fill in the blank spaces in the story.

Now you've created your own hilarious MAD LIBS® game!

CAN YOU TAKE THE HEAT?

ADJECTIVE _____

VERB ENDING IN "ING" _____

NOUN _____

NUMBER _____

NOUN _____

PLURAL NOUN _____

PLURAL NOUN _____

NOUN _____

PLURAL NOUN _____

NOUN _____

NOUN _____

ADJECTIVE _____

NOUN _____

NOUN _____

NOUN _____

ADJECTIVE _____

ADJECTIVE _____

ARTICLE OF CLOTHING _____

MAD LIBS
CAN YOU TAKE THE HEAT?

For some teams, winning boils down to one _____ formula—
  ADJECTIVE

pitching, _____, and more pitching. Today's hurlers
  VERB ENDING IN "ING"

can light up a radar _____, racking up 1-2-_____ innings
  NOUN   NUMBER

and leaving nothing but zeros on the score-_____. Noah
  NOUN

Syndergaard looks like the Norse god of _____ and inspires
  PLURAL NOUN

Mets fans to hang _____ in place of "K" signs. In Kansas
  PLURAL NOUN

City, Kelvin Herrera's heater can set off a/an _____ detector!
  NOUN

Facing Red Sox closer Craig Kimbrel? Forget rally _____.
  PLURAL NOUN

Bring a/an _____ extinguisher! And when flame thrower
  NOUN

Aroldis Chapman takes the hill, we've got two words: _____
  NOUN

over. More than ever, pitchers are dialing up their velocity. However,

throwing _____ cheddar is just half the _____. Pitch
  ADJECTIVE   NOUN

command separates an ordinary _____-slinger from a true
  NOUN

_____ in the rough. When Dodgers pitcher Clayton Kershaw
  NOUN

paints the _____ part of the plate with a/an _____
  ADJECTIVE   ADJECTIVE

slider, baffled batters swing right out of their _____!
  ARTICLE OF CLOTHING

MAD LIBS® is fun to play with friends, but you can also play it by yourself! To begin with, DO NOT look at the story on the page below. Fill in the blanks on this page with the words called for. Then, using the words you have selected, fill in the blank spaces in the story.

Now you've created your own hilarious MAD LIBS® game!

SLUGGERS AT THE CINEMA

TYPE OF LIQUID _____

OCCUPATION _____

NOUN _____

ADJECTIVE _____

TYPE OF FOOD _____

PERSON IN ROOM _____

ANIMAL _____

PLURAL NOUN _____

TYPE OF FOOD _____

VERB _____

ADJECTIVE _____

SILLY WORD _____

NOUN _____

VERB ENDING IN "ING" _____

TYPE OF FOOD _____

NOUN _____

NUMBER _____

FIRST NAME (MALE) _____

MAD LIBS
SLUGGERS AT THE CINEMA

So the game is in a/an _____ delay and your team's
TYPE OF LIQUID

_____ has rolled a giant _____ over the infield.
OCCUPATION NOUN

Why the _____ face? Pop a bag of _____ and enjoy
ADJECTIVE TYPE OF FOOD

one of these Hollywood classics!

The Sandlot: A group of friends must rescue a baseball signed by the

immortal _____ from the neighbor's dreaded _____.
PERSON IN ROOM ANIMAL

Field of _____: A farmer builds a ballpark in his _____
PLURAL NOUN TYPE OF FOOD

field when a voice says, "If you build it, he will _____."
VERB

Major League: The Indians' owner is sabotaging the team, but

Rick "_____ Thing" Vaughn and a voodoo power called
ADJECTIVE

_____ have other ideas.
SILLY WORD

A/An _____ *of Their Own*: Female ballplayers prove girls can
NOUN

play, too, even if there is no _____ in baseball!
VERB ENDING IN "ING"

Moneyball: General Manager Billy _____ thinks outside the
TYPE OF FOOD

_____ to build a contender.
NOUN

_____ *Men Out*: Players are bribed to throw the World Series.
NUMBER

Say it ain't so, _____!
FIRST NAME (MALE)

MAD LIBS® is fun to play with friends, but you can also play it by yourself! To begin with, DO NOT look at the story on the page below. Fill in the blanks on this page with the words called for. Then, using the words you have selected, fill in the blank spaces in the story.

Now you've created your own hilarious MAD LIBS® game!

THE SEVENTH INNING STRETCH

NOUN _____

NOUN _____

TYPE OF FOOD (PLURAL) _____

FIRST NAME (MALE) _____

VERB _____

VERB _____

ADJECTIVE _____

VERB _____

NOUN _____

NUMBER _____

ADJECTIVE _____

ADJECTIVE _____

NOUN _____

MAD LIBS
THE SEVENTH INNING STRETCH

Take me out to the _____-game.
NOUN

Take me out with the _____.
NOUN

Buy me some _____
TYPE OF FOOD (PLURAL)

and Cracker _____.
FIRST NAME (MALE)

I don't care if I ever _____ back.
VERB

Let me root, root, _____ for the _____ team.
VERB   ADJECTIVE

If they don't _____ it's a/an _____.
VERB   NOUN

For it's one, two, _____ strikes, you're _____
NUMBER   ADJECTIVE

at the _____ ball-_____!
ADJECTIVE   NOUN

From MLB MAD LIBS® • ™ and © Major League Baseball Properties, Inc. Published in 2017 by Price Stern Sloan, an imprint of Penguin Random House LLC, 345 Hudson Street, New York, NY 10014.

MAD LIBS® is fun to play with friends, but you can also play it by yourself! To begin with, DO NOT look at the story on the page below. Fill in the blanks on this page with the words called for. Then, using the words you have selected, fill in the blank spaces in the story.

Now you've created your own hilarious MAD LIBS® game!

THE MANAGER'S KEYS TO THE SEASON

ADJECTIVE _____

NOUN _____

ADJECTIVE _____

OCCUPATION _____

PLURAL NOUN _____

ADJECTIVE _____

ADJECTIVE _____

PART OF THE BODY (PLURAL) _____

NOUN _____

VERB _____

NOUN _____

ANIMAL _____

PERSON IN ROOM _____

PLURAL NOUN _____

ADJECTIVE _____

ARTICLE OF CLOTHING _____

NOUN _____

A/An _____ start is important, but remember—baseball is
    ADJECTIVE

a marathon, not a/an _____. Some days won't be our best,
               NOUN

and we'll need to have a/an _____ memory and forget about
               ADJECTIVE

it. My longtime _____ told me that baseball is a game
         OCCUPATION

of _____. If you do the _____ things right,
  PLURAL NOUN   ADJECTIVE

_____ things will happen. I've hammered that message into
 ADJECTIVE

my players' collective _____. We need to take
        PART OF THE BODY (PLURAL)

the hype with a grain of _____ and just _____ things
              NOUN   VERB

one _____ at a time. That said, I think our veteran leadership
    NOUN

makes us a dark _____ to win it all this year. Take our captain,
        ANIMAL

_____, for example. He dropped twenty _____
PERSON IN ROOM   PLURAL NOUN

in the offseason and reported to camp _____. For that effort,
                 ADJECTIVE

I take my _____ off and salute. If everyone works
    ARTICLE OF CLOTHING

that hard, we will be a well-oiled _____!
                NOUN

MAD LIBS® is fun to play with friends, but you can also play it by yourself! To begin with, DO NOT look at the story on the page below. Fill in the blanks on this page with the words called for. Then, using the words you have selected, fill in the blank spaces in the story.

Now you've created your own hilarious MAD LIBS® game!

HALL OF FAME SPEECH

CELEBRITY _____

ADJECTIVE _____

NOUN _____

ADJECTIVE _____

NOUN _____

NOUN _____

VERB ENDING IN "ING" _____

A PLACE _____

PLURAL NOUN _____

PLURAL NOUN _____

PLURAL NOUN _____

NOUN _____

ADJECTIVE _____

PLURAL NOUN _____

ADJECTIVE _____

TYPE OF LIQUID _____

EXCLAMATION _____

MAD LIBS®

HALL OF FAME SPEECH

Thank you, _____, for that _____ introduction
                  CELEBRITY   ADJECTIVE

speech. It brought a/an _____ to my eye. Never in my wildest
                              NOUN

dreams did I ever think my _____ face would end up on
                                  ADJECTIVE

a/an _____ hanging in Cooperstown. As a rookie, I couldn't
          NOUN

buy a/an _____ with a runner in _____
              NOUN   VERB ENDING IN "ING"

position. I envisioned playing Single-A ball in (the) _____ for
                                                        A PLACE

some team called the Fighting _____ for my entire career.
                                  PLURAL NOUN

Today, standing here among these legendary _____, I am
                                                  PLURAL NOUN

filled with nothing but _____. To my wife, who proves that
                            PLURAL NOUN

behind every great man is a greater _____; my teammates and
                                          NOUN

managers, who kept me _____ for 162 _____;
                            ADJECTIVE   PLURAL NOUN

and, of course, the fans—you are the _____ reason I left every
                                          ADJECTIVE

ounce of _____ out on that field. So one last time, let's
              TYPE OF LIQUID

hear that signature chant, "Hip hip . . . _____!"
                                              EXCLAMATION

Download Mad Libs today!

Join the millions of Mad Libs fans creating
wacky and wonderful stories on our apps!